PRAYING

the Jesus Prayer

ANCIENT SPIRITUAL DISCIPLINES

PRAYING
the Jesus Prayer

Frederica Mathewes-Green

PARACLETE PRESS
BREWSTER, MASSACHUSETTS

Praying the Jesus Prayer

2011 First Printing

Copyright © 2011 by Frederica Mathewes-Green

ISBN: 978-1-61261-059-7 (Pack of Five)

The Library of Congress has catalogued the original book *The Jesus Prayer*, from which this book is excerpted, as follows:

Mathewes-Green, Frederica.
  The Jesus prayer : the ancient desert prayer that tunes the heart to God / Frederica Mathewes-Green.
    p. cm.
  Includes bibliographical references.
  ISBN 978-1-55725-659-1
  1. Jesus prayer. I. Title.
  BT590.J28M38 2009
  242'.72—dc22

                                        2009025235

10 9 8 7 6 5 4 3 2 1

Published by Paraclete Press
Brewster, Massachusetts
www.paracletepress.com

Printed in the United States of America

CONTENTS

INTRODUCTION

It WAS ABOUT 2:30 IN THE MORNING when I got out of bed last night to pray. I have been doing this since I was pregnant with my first baby, decades ago; I had read somewhere that the middle of the night was a good time to have your daily prayers, with silence before and silence afterwards, and no phones to ring. I thought it sounded like a good habit to establish, since I'd be getting up with the baby anyway.

Over the years there were three babies, and eventually three teenagers, and now three young-marrieds with babies of their own. Now the household is down to my husband and me again. All these years I've been getting up in the night to pray. It's a necessity now, and I need it like I need food and light.

About fifteen years ago I started to use the Jesus Prayer during these mid-night hours: "Lord Jesus Christ, Son of God, have mercy on me." This very simple prayer was developed in the deserts of Egypt and Palestine during the early centuries of Christian faith, and has been practiced in the Eastern Orthodox Church ever since. It is a prayer inspired by St. Paul's exhortation to "pray constantly" (1 Thess. 5:17), and its purpose is to tune one's inner attention to the presence of the Lord.

But what is that nameless thing, the "inner attention"? When we talk about feeling God's presence, we're accustomed to speak as if such experiences arise from our emotions. Yet when I had my rather dramatic conversion experience, decades ago, it sure seemed more objective than that. At the time, the best way I could describe it was to say that "a little radio switched on inside me," and I became aware of Christ speaking to me. (It wasn't something I heard with my ears, but by an inner voice, filling my awareness.)

I never knew what to make of that "little radio"; it didn't fit our familiar division of people into "head" and "heart." But as I began to read the literature of Eastern Christianity, I found that they were familiar with this "little radio." They even had a word for it: the *nous*. It's a word that recurs through the Greek New Testament, but we don't have a good equivalent in English. It gets translated "mind," but it doesn't mean the talkative mind, the one that cogitates and constructs theories. It is a receptive capacity of the intellect; we could call it "the understanding" or "the comprehension." The Eastern Church has always known that the nous can be trained to register or perceive the voice of God.

That is where the Jesus Prayer comes in. The idea is to spend some time every day practicing the Prayer. You pray it fifty or a hundred times, or more, or less; not robotically but sincerely, speaking to Christ while pulling together your attention to the best of your ability. You get the Prayer going other times, too, whenever you think of it, while waiting at a stoplight or brushing your teeth. This brief, all-purpose, very portable prayer takes root and spreads.

In the process, you hone your ability to discern God's presence. He is already there, of course; we just aren't very good at perceiving it. Practicing the Jesus Prayer helps you sharpen your ability to "tune in" to his presence, just as you would practice scales to hone your ability to identify musical pitch.

So last night I awoke, as usual, without an alarm— sometime in the middle of the night I just swim up to consciousness. I went out into the hallway and stood on the worn spot in the carpet, in front of the bookcase, and looked up at the icon of Christ. A blue light was slanting in the window from my study, filtering between the large, heart-shaped leaves of the catalpa tree. Our street, a simple curve on a hilltop, was still. Sometimes, if I wake up later, I hear an early-rising robin robustly anticipating the dawn (and probably annoying all the other birds, who are still trying to get some shut-eye), but last night it was too early even for him.

I looked into the face of Christ, illuminated softly now by candlelight. I made the sign of the cross. I said some preliminary prayers, including the Lord's Prayer and the Nicene Creed, and recited Psalm 51, the prayer that David offered when he repented for seducing Bathsheba and murdering her husband. I've heard that you should "warm up your heart" before beginning the Jesus Prayer, and these preliminaries help do that; the Creed reminds me of the majesty of God, while Psalm 51 reminds me of my neediness, my damaged, greedy condition.

After that, I began repeating the Jesus Prayer in my mind, over and over, in an unhurried way: "Lord Jesus Christ, have mercy on me." (The words can be varied a bit; I use a shorter version, while the standard form is, "Lord Jesus Christ, Son of God, have mercy on me." My husband uses an even longer version, praying, "Lord Jesus Christ, Son of the Living God, have mercy on me, a sinner," the last phrase an echo of the tax collector's prayer in Jesus' parable.) I aim to say this prayer a hundred times, and keep track by moving my fingers along a prayer rope, a loop of silken cord tied with a hundred elaborate knots. When my mind wanders—which it does, believe me, over and over every night—I back up a few knots and focus in again.

This practice of saying the Jesus Prayer is accurately termed a spiritual discipline; it's a disciplined learning process, like learning to play the cello. It takes perseverance and focused attention. For a cellist, the tedium of practicing scales must appear so distant from the final goal, when that beautiful, dark music will spill forth fluidly. Yet, one day, the cellist will pick up her bow, and she and the instrument will have become one.

So I keep on asking Christ for mercy, working the Prayer deep into my awareness. I say it a hundred times at night, and throughout the day I set it going in my mind as often as I remember (hopefully, at least once an hour). But it is the focused mid-night prayer time that really enables it to root down deep.

And gradually I am coming to see that it is true. It really is possible to sense the presence of God— continuously.

I hasten to add that I *don't* sense it continuously. To be completely honest, I don't want to. I'd rather slide away into thinking about things that attract me, or anger me, or frighten me, and behave as if I can deal with them on my own. Apparently I think I can pull down a window shade between God and me, and do things the way I want to without him finding out. That's ridiculous, of course; if I turned my back on him and ran away as fast as I could, wherever I stopped he would have beaten me there. "Whither shall I go from thy Spirit? Or whither shall I flee from thy presence? If I ascend to heaven, thou art there! If I make my bed in Sheol, thou art there!" (Ps. 139:7–8).

But he is loving and very patient, and when I'm ready to turn and look at him again, I find that he has been continuing all that time to hold me in his steady gaze. Then the Prayer rises up inside, and makes a connection like a lamp plugging into a socket.

This prayer is not designed to generate fancy mystical experiences or soppy emotions. Yet it works away steadily inside, gradually building a sure connection with the Lord. Where the Lord enters in, there is light; I can see many ways that he has changed me over the years, illuminating and dispelling reflexive lying thoughts and fears. My part was just to keep showing up, day after day, for these quiet sessions with him.

The Prayer's goal is to help you keep always in touch with the presence of God. Some of you are already saying, "This is for me. This is what I've always wanted." You know what I mean by "the presence of God," because you've felt it yourself. And whether it was on one or two memorable occasions, or regularly over the years, you agree that it is intoxicating. When I try to describe it, I find I use the word *beauty* more often than any other. You know what I'm talking about, and you're eager to hear more.

But some of you feel sad when you hear people talk of such experiences. You've never felt anything you would describe as "the presence of God." You wonder why you've been left out. Has God rejected you?

The first thing I want to tell you is this: the very fact that you want to know God's presence means you're already sensing *something*. Think about it. How many people never give God a second thought? How many people sleep in on Sunday morning, and never open a Bible or send up a prayer? But you're not like that; you really want to be closer to the Lord. My hunch is that you are already sensing something of God's presence, or you wouldn't care.

Here's a homely analogy: picture yourself walking around a shopping mall, looking at the people and the window displays. Suddenly, you get a whiff of cinnamon. You weren't even hungry, but now you really crave a cinnamon roll. This craving isn't something you made up. There you were, minding your own business, when some drifting molecules of sugar, butter, and spice collided with a susceptible patch inside your nose. You had a real encounter with cinnamon—not a mental delusion, not an emotional projection, but the real thing.

And what was the effect? You want more, *now*. And if you hunger to know the presence of God, it's because, I believe, you have already begun to scent its compelling delight.

So, if you're one of those people who think that you've never had an experience of God, ask yourself: Why do you even care? Why do you spend time praying? Why do you bother to read the Bible, or books about prayer? The world is full of ways to waste your time. But if you picture yourself giving up on prayer, you feel hollow, desolated. All this must be doing *something*, even if you can't put your finger on it. The Prayer can help you learn to perceive that something, and do so more consistently and accurately.

About now some of you are thinking, "Well, I certainly have wandered into the wrong room." You don't recognize yourself here at all. You're not much for churchgoing. You're not even sure you would call yourself a Christian. But you do want to grow spiritually, and you want to know God better. Is it all right for you to use the Prayer too?

As we'll see, in the Christian East, homeland of the Jesus Prayer, there is some opinion that it can be harmful to practice the Jesus Prayer if you are not fully engaged in the life of the Orthodox Church, receiving the sacraments and guided by a wise spiritual elder. So if some think it's unwise even for non-Orthodox Christians to take up the Prayer, then it would certainly be too risky for a non-Christian to attempt it.

I don't expect those concerns will dissuade such readers who still want to try it, however. So I'll just give a word of advice. The spiritual realm is real, I have found, and not all the forces in it are benign. The less benign powers are associated, in particular, with lying (Jn. 8:44). This is a context, then, in which it is not wise to practice insincerity or hypocrisy. Perhaps you admire Jesus of Nazareth as an important historical figure and an eloquent teacher—but the Prayer commits you to more than that. The first word of the Prayer is *Lord*, a statement that you acknowledge Jesus of Nazareth as your Lord. Then you call him "Christ," from the Greek word meaning "Anointed One," or, in Hebrew, "the Messiah."

Those are some significant assertions, and if you don't agree with them, ask yourself why you *want* to pray the Prayer. You may feel that, for reasons you can't identify, it just seems to be calling to you. That is an interesting thing—in fact, it is a good thing. If you respond to that call with an open mind, you may reap something from the Prayer that you never expected.

There's one motivation for taking up the Prayer that I would discourage, though. Somehow in our day, the concept of "spirituality" has gotten unhitched from actual communion with God—and the fear and trembling authentic contact evokes—and come to be regarded almost as a hobby. Folks who seek spirituality rather than God can give off whiffs of superiority, as if they think they're more elevated than ordinary folks.

Once when I was speaking about the Prayer, a man in the audience commented, "Somehow this seems different from what I usually hear about spirituality. I think the main thing is that it doesn't have that element of narcissism."

The spiritual path of the Jesus Prayer is not one that lends itself to narcissism. The effect of the Prayer is to knock you down in your own mind. Then you discover that it is safe to be knocked down, safe to be humble, because God's love is everywhere, filling the world with his light and life. The Prayer will make you into a child. "Truly, I say to you, whoever does not receive the kingdom of God like a child shall not enter it" (Mk. 10:15). When defensiveness falls away and humility flows in, you become able to love others with the love that God has for them, and even "count others better than yourselves," as St. Paul urged the Philippians (Phil. 2:3).

I am hardly an expert on the Jesus Prayer, but I'd like to help you understand it at least as far as I do. Too many of us spend our days feeling that God is far away, occupied with more important things. But Jesus told us that isn't true; God is so familiar with our bodies that "even the hairs of your head are all numbered" (Matt. 10:30); he is so familiar with our thoughts that he "knows what you need before you ask him" (Matt. 6:8). I hope that through the Jesus Prayer you, too, may learn how to tune that "little radio" to the voice of God, and discover the joy of his infinitely loving presence.

CHAPTER ONE

History, Scripture, and the Meaning of Mercy

T HE JESUS PRAYER arose in the early church as a way to practice continuous prayer. When I decided to start using it in my own life, I remembered that St. Paul had said something about "pray constantly," and I went to look up that passage.

I was surprised to find that he had expressed the thought in four different places:

"Rejoice in your hope, be patient in tribulation, be constant in prayer." (Rom. 12:12)

"Pray at all times in the Spirit, with all prayer and supplication. To that end keep alert with all perseverance." (Eph. 6:18)

"Continue steadfastly in prayer, being watchful in it with thanksgiving." (Col. 4:2)

"Rejoice always, pray constantly, give thanks in all circumstances." (1 Thessalonians 5:16–18)

He must have thought this message was important, because he said it to four different communities—the Romans, Thessalonians, Ephesians, and Colossians. It must have been one of the points he emphasized regularly. And he must have thought it was possible. He wouldn't have kept on telling these early believers to "pray constantly" if they were humanly incapable of doing so.

It's not easy to do, though, is it? Many devout Christians have taken a stab at trying to pray constantly, but have given up in frustration before long. In my case, I was always discovering that somewhere along the line I had simply stopped praying. When I did persevere, I ran out of things to say. If I tried filling the time by just repeating, "Thank you, Lord," and such, it soon felt hollow. I worried that I was even ruining my ability to pray sincerely, numbing myself by repeating prayers without paying attention.

And, frankly, I just didn't understand how it was supposed to work. How can you be thinking prayers all the time, when you have to think about other things too?

Earlier generations of Christians figured all this out. In the third century, prayerful men and women began to go into the deserts of Egypt and Palestine in order to devote themselves unceasingly to communion with God. (They are known as the Desert Fathers and Mothers, and have the title "Abba" and "Amma.") The desert appealed to them because it eliminated most of those other things to think about, and life was stripped down to the essentials. Extreme deprivation taught self-mastery, and was itself a form of physical prayer.

In the desert, these spiritual athletes experimented with different forms of constant prayer. They recognized that the task was to discipline the wandering mind and focus it on something spiritually healthful, so they memorized the Scriptures (the Psalms, in particular) and quietly murmured the verses to themselves throughout the day.

Great depths could be found in a single line. Abba Pambo (AD 303–375) could not read, so he asked another desert dweller to teach him a psalm. When he heard the first words of Psalm 39, "I will guard my ways, that I may not sin with my tongue," he asked the other monk to stop and then meditated on that verse alone—for nineteen years. (Asked whether he was ready to hear at least the remainder of the verse, he replied that he had not mastered the first part yet.) Evagrius of Pontus (AD 345–399), on the other hand, listed 487 Scriptures, each of which was to be memorized and brought forth when needed to combat a specific temptation. St. John Cassian (AD 360–435) recommended the first verse of Psalm 70 as the best all-purpose Scripture for those seeking continual prayer: "Be pleased, O God, to deliver me! O Lord, make haste to help me!"

With time, the form "Lord Jesus Christ, Son of God, have mercy on me" emerged as the universal favorite. It echoes the many times people asked Jesus for mercy during the years of his earthly ministry:

"A Canaanite woman from that region came out and cried, 'Have mercy on me, O Lord, Son of David.'" (Matt. 15:22)

The ten lepers "lifted up their voices and said, 'Jesus, Master, have mercy on us.'" (Lk. 17:11–19) "Bartimaeus, a blind beggar, the son of Timaeus, was sitting by the roadside. And when he heard that it was Jesus of Nazareth, he began to cry out and say, 'Jesus, Son of

David, have mercy on me!' And many rebuked him, telling him to be silent; but he cried out all the more, 'Son of David, have mercy on me!'" (Mk. 10:46–48)

"A man came up to him and kneeling before him said, 'Lord, have mercy on my son, for he is an epileptic and he suffers terribly.'" (Mt. 17:14–15)

But what does it mean to ask for mercy? Some people feel uncomfortable with that plea, since asking for mercy over and over could sound like doubting God's forgiveness. Why do we have to keep begging, like a prisoner begging a judge to be lenient?

Take another look at these Scriptures. None are requests for leniency; all are cries for help. The pleas come from people who know that they are needy. Each one appeals to Jesus' compassion, his pity. The need may be for release from an illness, or release from the tyranny of sin. (We could add the tax collector in Jesus' parable, who "would not even lift up his eyes to heaven, but beat his breast, saying, 'God be merciful to me a sinner!'" Lk. 18:13.) In some way we don't immediately understand, healing and forgiveness are linked.

The roots of the Jesus Prayer go back to the early centuries of Eastern Christianity, and we can get a better understanding of what the Prayer means by examining how it works in that native context, and seeing how the Orthodox Church views sin and forgiveness. I am writing this book during Orthodox Holy Week, and just last night attended the service of Holy Unction, in which we consecrated the oil that will be used in anointing for healing during the coming

year. In the course of this service we heard seven
Epistle and seven Gospel readings, each presenting
examples of miraculous healing; we also offered many
prayers emphasizing God's compassion. After that,
the Gospel Book was held open over the heads of the
worshipers, who came forward to be anointed with the
newly blessed oil.

Throughout the evening, the theme of healing was
interwoven with assurance of forgiveness; we were
often reminded that those who are anointed have been
forgiven their sins as well. In a mystery, the two go
together; God's compassion to heal is his compassion
to forgive. We see an example of this in practice, when
Jesus says first to the paralytic lowered through the roof,
"Your sins are forgiven" (Matt. 9:2), healing his soul in
advance of healing his body.

The Eastern Christian tradition lays great stress
on God's willing forgiveness. Like the father of the
prodigal son, he longs for the sinner's return: "While
[the son] was yet at a distance, his father saw him and
had compassion, and ran and embraced him and kissed
him" (Lk. 15:20). God "desires all men to be saved and
to come to the knowledge of the truth" (1 Tim. 2:4).
Jesus said that "the Son of Man came to seek and to
save the lost" (Lk. 19:10), and "I came not to call the
righteous, but sinners" (Mk. 2:17). God spoke these
words through the prophet Ezekiel: "As I live, says
the Lord God, I have no pleasure in the death of the
wicked, but that the wicked turn from his way and live;
turn back, turn back from your evil ways; for why will

you die?" (Ezek. 33:11). Orthodox prayers regularly call God "all-compassionate," "all-merciful," and state, "you alone love mankind." God's love is the only love in the universe worthy of the name. God is love, and his forgiveness can be nothing but abundant and free.

So this isn't a question about whether we're forgiven. No, the problem lies elsewhere; the problem is *we keep on sinning*. Sin is in us like an infection in the blood. It keeps us choosing to do and say and think things that damage Creation and hurt other people—and the ill effects rebound on us as well. There can even be sin without guilt. Sometimes we add to the weary world's burden of sin through something we did in ignorance or unintentionally, for example, by saying something that hurt a hearer for reasons we knew nothing about. Our words increased the sin-sickness in the world, yet we are not guilty for that unintentional sin (though we are still sorry for inadvertently causing pain). Sin can be recognized as a noxious force on earth without having to pin the guilt on someone every time.

In the Eastern view, all humans share a common life; when Christ became a member of the human race, our restoration was begun. The opposite is, sadly, true as well; our continuing sins infect and damage everybody else, and indeed Creation itself. It's like air pollution. There is suffering for everyone who shares our human life, everyone who breathes, even the innocent who never did anyone harm.

The devil is implicated in this pattern. This is a premodern church, and Orthodox Christians retain a practical belief in the devil, one rooted in long experience. The evil one is a tempter, rather than a figure from a horror movie; his goal is to destroy our faith and drag us from salvation. And he loves suffering, especially when it is inflicted on the innocent. That's two-for-one, in his book; he gets to savor not only the tears and agony of the innocent, but also the distress of us not-so-innocent folks who look on helplessly. If he handles things just right, and suggests the right desolating thought at the optimal moment, he might even undermine an onlooker's faith in God.

In the Christian East there is an answer to the problem of evil: "An enemy has done this" (Matt. 13:28). And our own petty sins contribute to his strength.

So we ask for mercy because we are sick with sin, and will go on sinning. Even though we are as confident as beloved children in our Father's compassion, we grieve because we contribute more to the planet's suffering every day. The tragedies in each morning's news were assisted in some small way by yesterday's stupid, selfish, fearful choices. We are helplessly entangled in sin and suffering, and only Jesus' touch will heal us. We cry out with the blind, lame, and paralyzed of his day: Lord Jesus Christ, have mercy on us!

God doesn't need us to remind him to be merciful; he is merciful all the time, even when we don't ask. But unless we make a habit of asking for mercy, we forget that we *need* it. Ego builds a cardboard fortress that humility must, every day, tear down. "For you say, I am rich, I have prospered, and I need nothing; not knowing that you are wretched, pitiable, poor, blind, and naked" (Rev. 3:17). We are pitiable, and God pities us. With God's merciful help, we begin to heal. Progress is not very discernible in the midst of the fray, but over time it becomes clear that we are indeed fighting off the infection and gradually getting stronger, less fretful, more loving. With the Jesus Prayer, we begin to get some breathing room. We start to be able to recognize the subtle thoughts that lead toward temptation, before it is too late and they overwhelm us. We see and resist them, and every such victory increases our strength to resist next time.

Of course, sometimes we see those temptations and fall anyway. But even failures can work for our good. They induce genuine humility; they help us learn the devil's strategies; and they teach firsthand compassion for fellow sinners.

This process of healing takes a long time. Even as we see reasons for hope, we simultaneously gain better understanding of how far down the roots of sin can go. It would be devastating to see the whole truth about ourselves all at once. Our compassionate Lord brings us along gently, allowing some blissful ignorance. Each layer of the onion is shed at the right time; we encounter the next truth about ourselves when and how we can bear it, as our loving Lord knows best. "I have yet many things to say to you, but you cannot bear them now" (Jn. 16:12).

You can see why, if there was only one prayer you were going to continually offer, one that asked Jesus for

mercy would be ideal. The Prayer trains you to adopt
the stance of asking for mercy, because that is the pos-
ture from which you can best see his face. It's like trying
to see a star out your window on a summer night. The
leaves of the trees and the neighbors' roofs block your
view, but if you lean over just right and crane your neck
you can see it. The Jesus Prayer teaches you how to
"lean just right," combining joy, trust, penitence, and
gratitude, so you can find yourself in his presence.

Till now we've been talking about learning to sense
God's presence, but his plan for us goes even further
than that. We don't merely encounter Christ or imitate
him, we don't merely become like Christ; we actually
become one with him, saturated body and soul with his
life. It will be for us as it was for St. Paul: "For to me to
live is Christ" (Phil. 1:21), and, "It is no longer I who
live, but Christ who lives in me" (Gal. 2:20).

Have we gotten used to taking such words as pious
metaphor? In the Jesus Prayer tradition, they're simple
Bible truth. The whole point of salvation is restored
union with God. Christ came to rescue us from our
bondage to sin and the devil ("The reason the Son of
God appeared was to destroy the works of the devil,"
1 Jn. 3:8), and we are now free to grow in union with
him.

What could "union with God" mean, in practice? It
meant something different to me at one time than it
does now. Before my family and I joined the Eastern
Orthodox Church, in 1993, we were members of a
mainline liturgical church. I liked learning about the

historic faith (I'd gotten a seminary degree alongside my husband, a pastor) and did a good bit of reading in classic Western Christian spirituality. From the perspective I gained there, I associated talk about union with God with images of the mystic saints, floating above the ground and dizzy with ecstatic visions. That was the sort of stuff you left to professionals—the "don't try this at home" category of spirituality.

So it was surprising to find that, in the Eastern Christian tradition, union with God is the goal for everyone. It is God's will for every Christian, and, through their preaching of the gospel, for every human being. The purpose of this earthly life is to be saturated with the life of Christ. Everything flows from that, every work of art and act of courageous witness, every theological insight and every effort to help the poor. The idea is that God will fill people with his Son's life, and then they will accomplish his work in the world. It works better that way, actually. The other way round, when people set out to do things for God under their own steam, leads to disappointment, conflict, and wasted effort.

This process of assimilating the presence of God is called *theosis* (pronounced "THEH-o-sis"). *Theos* means "God," and as a cloth soaks up water by osmosis, we are saturated with God through *theosis*. This indwelling presence heals, restores, and completes us, preparing each of us to take up the role in his kingdom that we alone can fill.

Progress in *theosis* is a gift of God, not won by any effort, of course. But you can make yourself available to such a blessing by practicing spiritual disciplines, such as observing the fast days in the church's calendar (in the Orthodox Church, this means keeping a vegan diet) and saying the Jesus Prayer. Such resources are like the workout machines in a health club, the ones every serious athlete will use. People who are making progress share some common characteristics, too: good self-control when it comes to the appetites, absence of anger, ample humility, kindness, and diligence in prayer. But some folks have a more sober quality, while others are full of joy; there isn't any one personality type. If anything, the indwelling Christ enables each person to be more himself than he was ever able to be before.

I've noticed that men are particularly drawn to Eastern Christian spirituality. Men, I think, are starving for a form of Christianity that will ask something of them. They're hungry for a challenge—a *clear, straightforward* challenge, that is. I did an informal survey not long ago, asking male converts what had attracted them to Orthodoxy. I was surprised at how many men voiced gratitude, not just for the rigor of Eastern spirituality (*challenge* was, in fact, the most-used term), but also for the fact that expectations are set forth clearly, with no secret meanings that they have to figure out. Men are glad to do hard things, as long as they have a clear idea of what they're supposed to do. (In this gratitude for clarity I heard an echo of all the frustrated husbands who have said to their wives: "I'm not a mind reader—just tell me what you want!")

When this concept of *theosis* is unfamiliar, it is hard
for a reader to make any sense of it; it may even sound
alarming or kooky, or like empty, well-meaning piety.
Once I had given a talk about the Jesus Prayer at a
college, and as I left the podium a student was waiting
to ask me something, ready to jot down my answer. He
asked, "Are there any case histories?" I was perplexed by
the question, so he tried again: "Has anyone ever tried
to do this?"

I didn't say, "Well, *I'm* trying to do it." Instead, I
suggested a couple of names he could look up on the
Internet (St. Seraphim and Motovilov, in case you want
to look them up, too). But the moment impressed me
with how hard it must be to grasp what I'm talking
about from an isolated lecture or a book.

The Jesus Prayer isn't designed to be learned that
way. Historically, it has been passed on face-to-face,
from one Christ-loving person to the next, down the
generations from the time of the Desert saints. It is
learned in a community of fellow believers, all of whom
are aware of their need and sin, trying daily to resist
temptation better and love God more. It should be
individually coached or tutored by a spiritual mother or
father who knows you through and through, who loves
you, holds you accountable, and is able wisely to adapt
the classic teaching to your unique struggles. In short,
the Jesus Prayer is meant to be learned in the midst
of a living community, where you can see numerous
examples of what it looks like when ordinary people are
doing it and encouraging each other. When you can see

real folks doing it, it is a lot easier to grasp, and seems a lot more possible.

Theosis is a vast and daunting goal even to imagine, so there's something distinctively, sweetly Christian about using a prayer that is so simple. There have been plenty of other religions that taught convoluted mystical procedures for union with God, but for Christians it is as straightforward as calling on our Lord and asking him for mercy. As you form the habit of saying this prayer in the back of your mind all the time, it soaks into you, like dye into cotton, and colors the way you encounter every person and circumstance you meet.

There's the answer to the practical question I had a while back: how can you think about the words of the Prayer all the time, when there are so many other things you have to think about? In the same way that you can have a meal, go on a trip, or visit a museum with a friend. You could do all of those things alone, but if you take a friend with you, it won't hinder your enjoyment. You may get even more out of it, because your friend's presence enhances your awareness, and you see things through his eyes as well. When you see everything alongside that best of friends, Jesus Christ, your encounters with the world and everyone and everything in it are transformed.

CHAPTER TWO

Heart, Mind,
and the "Little Radio"

THE WAY TO DO THE JESUS PRAYER is to just keep saying it over and over. The instructions could fit on the back of a shampoo bottle:

1. Pray "Lord Jesus Christ, Son of God, have mercy on me."
2. Repeat.

But if that's all you know, you'll soon run into trouble. You can try to force your mind to keep going over and over those words, like a gerbil on a wheel, but it's going to get pretty tedious.

The hard part is to *mean* them. The hard part is to pull together all your attention, though it kicks like a toddler, and focus it on the Lord, and then humbly ask for his mercy. Learning to actually mean the Jesus Prayer, from ever-deepening regions of your heart, is what makes the practice so challenging.

What makes it so rewarding, however, is that you can begin to sense the responsive presence of the Lord. Then the words of the Prayer start to make sense—they start to feel like the natural thing to say. It's like saying,

"I love you." An adolescent can try to imagine how it will feel when he finally speaks those words to his true love, but no matter how much he practices, they remain mere words. When the moment comes, the experience of his beloved's presence is so overpowering that the words flow naturally, and seem like the only possible thing to say. They are no longer theoretical and portentous, but have become evidence of something piercingly real but inexpressible, vast beyond words.

One of the biggest handicaps we have in prayer, though, is that we aren't sure it's actually *possible* to sense the presence of God. That's the first thing we have to clear up, the assumption that we don't have the equipment necessary to perceive God's presence. If we want to perceive or sense something, we employ the standard equipment: sight, touch, hearing, and so on. But we don't expect God to manifest himself by such means. Talk of that kind of overt experience of God serves mostly to make the person talking look like a kook.

Apart from that, we think we have the two modes of active awareness. There's the "head," the intellect or human reason; we think of it as the side that is accurate and realistic, though a bit cold. In the opposite corner we have the "heart," which we see as an unstable swamp of emotions, though nevertheless the source of our finest impulses.

We like to say, "We need both head and heart." When talking with atheists, we're inclined to grant that they have "head" on their side, that their approach is more objective, or even scientific. We'd agree that when we experience the presence of God, it is a matter of our emotions, arising from the "heart." Thus we function under the assumption that there are two aspects of human consciousness, reason and emotion—and there's the problem. If we believe that God cannot be experienced through human reason, what's left for such contact to be but emotional? Thus, when you say you had an experience of God, it seems to mean that you had emotions about God.

It frustrates me that Christians so readily give way when this question comes up. If I said I experienced going to the dentist, you would assume that I actually went to the dentist. You wouldn't think I had some emotions that felt just like going to the dentist. It's only when we Christians begin talking about God that we get uncertain about how real it is and start agreeing with nonbelievers that "experience" means "emotional projection."

Once you start looking at it, though, this whole division into "head" and "heart" becomes less certain. If you think about your own inner life, you'll notice that "head" and "heart" aren't really polar opposites. In practice, they muddle up so much that they're impossible to separate. Emotions slip around our thoughts and shape them; "rational" is cousin to "rationalize." The way we want things to be can powerfully affect our ability to see how things really are.

And thoughts provoke strong emotions; it can be argued that *all* our emotions are reactions to thoughts. When you feel sad or excited, it's generated by something you're thinking about. Even when we can't put our finger on the cause of an emotion, somewhere behind it is foggy, perhaps suppressed, thought.

This insight, in fact, has produced a breakthrough in the treatment of psychological illness. It seemed that people could talk for years about their experiences and feelings, yet gain little improvement. More recently, some therapists have been trying a different approach: they encourage their clients to focus on their thoughts, rather than their emotions, with the aim of observing and challenging the erroneous ideas that provoke their anxiety or depression. The Prayer, as we'll see, utilizes a similar approach, calling us to be vigilant about the thoughts we harbor, scrutinizing them and rejecting lies. We know who the "father of lies" is (Jn. 8:44).

So, in practice, neither head nor heart is as airtight as we generally presume. This polarized picture of "head" and "heart" doesn't correspond to Scripture, either. There the word *head* is never used as a synonym for "reason." A glance at a Bible concordance will show that it always means either the physical head on a body or a person in authority, and never the rational intellect. Now, every culture certainly gets an opportunity to observe that head injury affects the ability to think, and from that must draw some conclusions about the cogitating function of the brain. Nevertheless, in the world of the Bible, the head is never associated with thinking.

Confusingly enough, the authors of Scripture, and Jesus himself, presume that thoughts arise instead in the *heart*. As Jesus said, "For out of the heart come evil thoughts" (Matt. 15:19). The association of the heart with thinking appears consistently throughout the Scriptures (as seen, for example, in Gen. 6:5, Ps. 33:11, Ps. 139:23, Jer. 4:14, Mk. 7:21, Lk. 2:35, and Heb. 4:12).

Feelings of tenderness and compassion, which we think of as synonymous with "heart" (as in, "That guy has a big heart") are instead associated with the contents of the abdomen and lower body: bowels, kidneys, womb, and the "inner parts" in general. (Here are some examples, though in contemporary translations the reference has often been euphemized: Matt. 15:32, 18:27, 20:34; Mk. 1:41, 8:2, 9:22; Lk. 1:78; 2 Cor. 6:12, 7:15; Phil. 1:8, 2:1; Col. 3:12; Philem. 1:7, 12, 20; 1 Jn. 2:17.)

So what used to be assigned to bowels and heart is now located in heart and mind. Apparently, over the last several millennia, everything's been rising.

Sometimes translators take it upon themselves to elevate the site of this inner attention just a little farther. The ancient Greek version of Psalm 16:7 reads, "I will bless the Lord who has given me understanding; in the night also my kidneys instruct me." The King James Version says, "My reins also instruct me," *reins* being an archaic term for "kidneys." The Revised Standard Version says, "In the night also my *heart* instructs me," while the New American Standard Version renders it, "My *mind* instructs me in the night." In another century, maybe we'll read, "My hat instructs me"!

When we say "mind" or "head," we think of the active process of reason—the part of us that builds theories and crafts arguments. The Greek word for that faculty is *dianoia* (pronounced "dthee-AN-nee-ah"). We don't have a word in English for the mental function when it goes the other direction, the part of us that confronts life firsthand, which perceives or comprehends. Since there's no word for it, we don't know it exists.

But it does exist, and in the Greek Scriptures, there's a word for it. When you see the word *mind* in an English Bible, the Greek word that lies behind it is usually *nous* (the "ou" as in "could"), and it doesn't quite equal our concept of "mind."

What it does mean was hard for me to figure out. When I began reading works about prayer from the Christian East, I noticed that *nous* was frequently left untranslated. This suggested that the English language just doesn't have a good equivalent. As I traveled around the country giving talks, meeting people who were trying to acquire the Prayer, they'd sometimes ask, "Do you understand what *nous* means?"

So I tried to nail it down. As I read through a lengthy book on Eastern Orthodox spirituality, I took an index card and wrote down the definition of *nous*, as best I could grasp it, every time I ran across the term. At the end of the book, I had six definitions.

But gradually I came to grasp that the kind of "mind" intended by *nous* primarily indicates the *receptive* faculty of the mind, what we might call "the understanding." For example, "[Jesus] opened their nous to understand the scriptures" (Lk. 24:45). This is the part of the mind that engages directly with life, which comprehends and takes things in.

What's more, it is a *perceptive* faculty, capable of recognizing truth. Not in the sense of arriving at a logical conclusion at the end of an argument; the nous instead perceives truth in a direct, intuitive way. When you hear "the ring of truth," it is your nous that does the resonating.

Another function of the nous is the ability to hear the conscience, that "little voice inside." You know you're not just talking to yourself, because it's telling you things that you would rather not hear. The nous keeps a line open to the voice of God and, even in a person who has wandered far from faith, a flickering link endures in the form of the (perhaps unwillingly) listening conscience.

So the nous enables a direct experience of God, apart from reason and emotion. But here's how we get tangled up: if you have an experience of the presence of God, it's quite likely you'll have thoughts and emotions *afterward*. But if your language doesn't provide a way to express the experience itself, and all you have words for is the emotions and thoughts that resulted, you're likely to assume that the experience itself was a function of your intellect or (more likely) emotions.

That's not the case. There really is an experience in the first place.

The nous is primarily a receiver—it's the "little radio" I lacked words for, just after my conversion. It is placed in us so that we can perceive God's voice and presence.

But in the Fall the nous was damaged—the usual term is "darkened"—and no longer perceives accurately. It doesn't much *want* to listen to God. It constantly craves stimulation. If you tried to keep track of your thoughts for even one hour you'd be amazed at their restless range. A contemporary elder said that the nous is like a dog that wants to run around all the time.

The nous needs healing. It doesn't perceive things clearly, due to damage caused by the fog of sin that affects us all. Healing of the nous involves getting rid of the erroneous thoughts and emotions that cloud our minds. We need to have a clear-eyed view of reality, if we want to encounter God. Reality is God's home address.

But the nous doesn't want to focus on the Prayer. When you start to pray, it gets restless and begins to jump around, trying to find anything at all to think about. The strangest thoughts pop in. In Greek, these attacking thoughts are called *logismoi* (pronounced "law-yiz-MEE"); a single thought is a *logismos*. (You'll hear such words pronounced in various ways. On the advice of Metropolitan Kallistos Ware, I am trying to use modern Greek pronunciation.)

Our thoughts about the world are what control us, and much of the time they are off base. You may be governed, unaware, by misunderstandings you picked up as a child. Thoughts about other people are especially likely to be erroneous and self-damaging. These false thoughts make us fearful, greedy, and vindictive; they undermine our trust in God, and make us subject to every kind of human dysfunction. The "darkened" nous is easily deluded, and self-deluded. The process of spiritual healing cleanses the nous, like cleaning grime off the glass of a lantern.

Here is where the Prayer comes in. With regular use, it begins to open up a little space between you and your automatic thoughts, so that you can scrutinize them before you let them in. It builds a foyer, so to speak, where incoming thoughts must wait to be examined before being granted admittance. This is a lifelong process, and your self-serving thoughts, in particular, are adept at disguising themselves; they may escape detection for many long years. But over time you will discover that some very old automatic thoughts are just plain wrong, and you don't have to think them anymore. As the nous is gradually healed, its perceptions become more accurate, less agitated. You begin to acquire "the nous of Christ" (1 Cor. 2:16). "Be transformed by the renewal of your nous," said St. Paul (Rom. 12:2).

So the Prayer has a great deal to do with your thoughts, your interior mental life. It will end up sending you, like an explorer, through the jungle of your own psyche. You will always be discovering something new about yourself, something you need to correct or move out of the way. In his book *The Sign of the Cross*, Andreas Andreopoulos described this process. "The individual's spiritual battle . . . is fought on many levels of the self, and is successful when the deepest parts of the personality have come to also reflect the spiritual struggle that the Cross attests. The Desert Fathers were very aware of this. Most of the ascetic literature essentially represents a sophisticated psychological journey into the self, with Jesus as the compass."[1] And also, I would add, the goal.

You can see why there is so much emphasis within Orthodoxy on having an elder, a spiritual guide. But many of us must, of necessity, take up this journey without an elder, and must therefore do so with fear and trembling. We must never forget that our heart is a nest of trickery and self-deception. "The heart is deceitful above all things, and desperately corrupt; who can understand it?" (Jer. 17:9). It is unable to perceive clearly: "a veil lies over their heart" (2 Cor. 3:15; this is another case where the Greek says "heart" but the English translation substitutes "mind"). It is possible, in the absence of an elder, to be led by the Holy Spirit. But it is wise to keep seeking for the one who can guide you with wise words and protect you with ardent prayer.

Be certain that there is no help in intellectuality, or in having read a great number of spiritual books. A common tragedy is for a person to get diverted from the path of prayer onto the path of *talking about* prayer. A sign that the enemy has penetrated far into the mind of such a one is that she becomes smug and no one can tell her anything. No attribute of intelligence or cleverness will save you, no ability to phrase things deftly, no elegant symmetry of your ideas. Just keep crying out for mercy. Only humility breaks in pieces all the machinery of the enemy.

We are like the prodigal son, who comes home sick and injured. It was his own sins that brought him to that state, and he can't blame anybody else. He repents because he now sees the truth. He doesn't need to repent in order to earn the father's forgiveness; the father had already forgiven him, and rushes forward to embrace his child without waiting to hear an apology. "While he was yet at a distance, his father saw him and had compassion" (Lk. 15:20).

God loves us like that; he isn't waiting for us to coax him into forgiving us. But, like the son, we have to recognize the truth about our wounded condition. We must recognize that we *need* the father's love. The darkened nous doesn't readily grasp this. We see that something is wrong with the world, but don't perceive that the wrongness is tangled up with, and enabled by, our own thoughts, words, and deeds. Realizing the truth about ourselves, our complicity in the world's broken-ness, is the first step of healing.

The prodigal son had that moment of clear insight; "he came to himself" (Lk. 15:17). Then he knew that he needed to go home and tell his father that he was sorry, and beg for a second chance.

Did the son have an emotional experience? No doubt about it; but it was the fruit of a moment of intellectual clarity. His understanding was enlightened, his nous recognized truth, he became rational; he was at last put in touch with reality.

The root meaning of *repentance*, or *metanoia* (pronounced "meh-TAN-ee-ah") in Greek, means that sort of change of mind: gaining insight, coming to your senses, seeing the truth. Jesus said, "You will know the truth, and the truth will make you free" (Jn. 8:32). It is hard to do that when you feel alone in the universe, with a distant God who doesn't know your name and may be sulking over something you did years ago. You can feel brave enough to know and admit this truth only when you are sure you are loved, because "perfect love casts out fear" (1 Jn. 4:18).

A God who is remote and scary and judgmental, taking offense at things that (we think) have nothing to do with him, is hard to love. The natural reaction is instead to deny the sins, or rationalize them away, or compare yourself to someone else whose behavior is worse. A barrier of mistrust lies between a person and this kind of God.

This Eastern Christian path is not particularly concerned with morality or good behavior, surprisingly enough; it is concerned with a *relationship*. The Pharisees achieved high levels of good behavior, but if that was enough, Jesus would have chosen his apostles from their ranks. No, they were pretty on the outside and rotten on the inside, like "whitewashed tombs" (Matt. 23:27). Jesus consistently put the emphasis on the state of the inner person. He said, for example, that the eating of "unclean" foods does not defile a person, but rather what comes out of the mouth, because that rises from the heart: "evil thoughts, murder . . . false witness, slander" (Matt. 15:19).

It's that transformed heart and nous he's looking for. After that healing, good behavior flows out naturally. So this approach does not disregard morality; Jesus said, "You, therefore, must be perfect, as your heavenly Father is perfect" (Mt. 5:48), and "Unless your righteousness exceeds that of the scribes and Pharisees, you will never enter the kingdom of heaven" (Matt. 5:20). But moral behavior is worthless without a transformed mind and heart. To get good fruit, you must "make the tree good" (Matt. 12:33).

That's the kind of repentance God is looking for—a change deep inside us, one that signals our desire to restore the relationship and be conformed to his likeness. This healing is premised on the confidence that God already sees all the way through us. He sees everything we ever did, knows our every thought, and yet loves us, even enough to die for us. So there is no reason to hide and make excuses; he already knows it all, anyway. Remember the story in the Gospels, in which Jesus was at supper at the home of Simon the Pharisee and a penitent woman came in and wept at his feet, washing them with her tears. As Jesus told Simon, she had great love, because she knew she had been forgiven much.

Those who think of themselves as fairly decent and upright are going to have a harder time achieving repentance. Such a person doesn't see that God has had to forgive very much in them. As a result, they can't be sure that his love is strong. Those who are forgiven much, love much; they know they are receiving much love.

The practice of the Prayer will initially take some serious self-discipline, but it gradually grows sweet, and then irresistible. The hope of protection from your own vicious or self-hating thoughts is alone a strong impetus to persevere. Day by day the healing advances, and continual immersion in Christ's presence becomes your goal. One day you will find that the Prayer is starting up within you on its own, like a dearly loved melody. And then you will know the blessing that St. Paul gave the Philippians, "the peace of God, which overflows all the nous, will keep your *kardia* [hearts] and *noema* [thoughts] in Christ Jesus" (Phil. 4:7).

CHAPTER THREE

Getting Started

Orthodox elders would say that you must first get your house in order. If there is major ongoing sin in your life, then cut it out. At least *want* to cut it out; cultivate repentance by thinking on the glory and compassion of God, and your squandering of that love. It is actually better to repent sincerely of a sin, and to go on struggling even though you fall, than to have never had the temptation in the first place. Jesus said, "There will be more joy in heaven over one sinner who repents than over ninety-nine righteous persons who need no repentance" (Lk. 15:7). The sinner who doesn't repent is another matter.

Look for a spiritual mother or father. Many Orthodox Christians turn to their parish priest for this, while others seek one at a men's or women's monastery. If you can't find one, embark on the Jesus Prayer with whatever resources you can gather, but retain an extra measure of caution about your own capacity for spiritual pride. You're still bound to make some mistakes, but at least you won't be surprised when you do.

Attend worship; be part of a worshiping community. Receive the sacraments (in Orthodoxy, called "Holy Mysteries"). Go to confession, if that is part of your spiritual heritage.

Pray, fast, and give alms. Eastern Christians continue the first-century practice of fasting on Wednesday and Friday, and during Great Lent and other fast periods during the year. This is not an absolute fast, but mostly a matter of abstaining from meat, fish, and dairy. Give a tenth of your income, a tithe, to your church, if you can; if not, give whatever percentage you can afford and work up to (and then beyond) the tithe. Give alms to charity as well. Give wisely.

Serve those in sorrow and need, in person if at all possible, for personal contact will affect you in ways not gained through merely writing a check. In our culture we are disposed to approach social needs with an eye to efficiency, expecting to pool expertise and resources, form an organization, and execute a program. The achievements of such organizations are so substantial that what we do privately tends to look insignificant. But the Scriptures presume that all charity is taking place in the context of personal relationships.

Our word charity comes from the Latin caritas, corresponding to the Greek New Testament word agape, which means "long-suffering, self-giving love." This is the kind of love we are supposed to show to the poor and needy. In fact, we should give that love even to those who are not poor and needy; we're supposed to love everyone, even our persecutors (Lk. 6:27–28).

So practice agape in every context (and it does take lots of practice). Every person you encounter gives you a God-appointed opportunity to die to self. The six or ten people you deal with every day are meant to furnish your own personal "Roman Coliseum," where you can battle against self-will till your last breath. The elders are unanimous that curbing self-will, dying to self at every opportunity, is essential to spiritual healing and growth. This kind of self-discipline is called asceticism, after the Greek word for the training an athlete undergoes when preparing for a marathon, or an apprentice follows in learning her craft. Asceticism is not hatred of the body. The body's inborn, natural desires are good when they operate as God intended, but in practice they tend to overrun their boundaries. Sometimes the mind even exceeds the body's desires, as when I eat something because it says "chocolate" on the wrapper, even though it doesn't taste particularly good. As the nous is cleansed and strengthened, it will be more able to guide the body rightly.

It is standard advice to avoid excessive sleeping, and to leave the table before you feel full. Overeating is widely recognized as a factor that undermines the ability to maintain constant prayer. Continually stretch yourself with small challenges in all areas of your preferences and desires, cutting away little pleasures that you think you can't live without. But don't go overboard with a sudden, possibly prideful, attempt at excessive asceticism. This seems to tempt young men more than it does other people. "One needs to get used to moderation gradually" says Abp. Anthony Golynsky-Mihailovsky (AD 1889–1976).[2]

Expect that you will have sorrow, and that you will suffer injustice; expect this, and it won't shatter your faith. Believe firmly that all your joy is with Christ, and you will be able to bear it if other sources of joy prove temporary, or are never found at all. And keep in mind that our sins assist the evil one and contribute to the world's ongoing tragedy, so it is fitting that we bear part of the resulting burden.

Jesus said, "In the world you have tribulation." You will, he promises; just take a deep breath, and accept it. In this world, pain will visit everyone sooner or later.

But Jesus didn't stop with that thought. He went on, "But be of good cheer, I have overcome the world" (Jn. 16:33). Pain may be inevitable, but it is also temporary, and that alone is a comforting thought. Pain is mandatory, but misery is optional.

Humility is of more value than the greatest asceticism. One day, as the desert monk St. Macarius (AD 300–391) was returning to his cell, the devil attacked him swinging a scythe, but was unable to wound him. The devil complained, "Macarius, I suffer a lot of violence from you, for I cannot overcome you. Whatever you do, I do also. If you fast, I eat nothing; if you keep watch, I never sleep. There is only one way in which you surpass me: your humility. That is why I cannot prevail against you."

Pride can be hard to detect because it disguises itself in innumerable ways. It appears most often in relationships, because pride springs up when comparing yourself with other people. If you instead compare yourself with God, and with what God is calling and enabling you to be, sincere humility is not so hard to feel.

One clue to pride is anger; often, when we get angry, it is because pride has been dealt a wound. Avoid anger at all costs. The Desert Fathers warn more frequently against anger than against sexual sins, because anger poisons the soul. As the saying goes, "Anger is an acid that destroys its container." Consider yourself too immature to handle even so-called "righteous anger." More frequently, this turns out to be self-righteous anger. Jesus was able to roar into the temple and throw tables over, but he had certain spiritual advantages that we don't. Our popular entertainment routinely invites us to indulge in vicarious vengeance, and presents it as a noble and satisfying pursuit. But "you did not so learn Christ" (Eph. 4:20), for our Lord could have called down "more than twelve legions of angels" (Matt. 26:53) and orchestrated a very cinematic vengeance, if that was his way of doing things.

It's a long list, and no one is going to do it all perfectly. Still, Jesus said, "You, therefore, must be perfect, as your heavenly Father is perfect" (Matt. 5:48), so we should keep pressing onward. Do whatever you can to make your soul "pleasant to God," as Fr. Surioanu so gently recommended. Every failure can be turned to gold, if it increases your humility.

Q: AND THEN WHAT?
HOW DO I BEGIN THE PRAYER ITSELF?

The goal is to gain the Jesus Prayer as an unceasing prayer offering to God. It sounds lofty, but as with so many of the worthwhile things in life, a large part of meeting your goal depends on just showing up. Do what you said you'd do, whether you feel like it or not. Simple perseverance eventually succeeds, like water wearing away a stone.

In basic terms, what you're attempting to do is to form a new habit. In this case, it's the habit of praying without ceasing. Yet, due to the restlessness and distractibility of our minds, an attempt to start out praying right now and never stop is going to be met with disappointment.

It's impossible to start doing anything *all* the time. You have to start with doing it *some* of the time. Set aside a regular time for practice every day, and as the habit takes root you can encourage it to spread out from there, like vines escaping the boundaries of a garden.

The first thing to decide is when you're going to have this practice time. Perhaps you already have a daily "quiet time," during which you pray, read the Bible, offer intercessions, and so forth. You can add to that time an extra ten or fifteen minutes for repeating the Jesus Prayer. You could even undertake one prayer session in the morning and the other in the evening, and set the Prayer going once again as you drop off to sleep. However, don't set your sights too high; establish goals that you can reasonably keep. You can always add more later.

I found that the single biggest advance in my prayer life came when I expanded from my single mid-night prayer time and added brief "prayer stops" during the day at morning, noon, sunset, and bedtime. Those prayer times were never for me as deep and rich as the mid-night session, but the mere act of breaking up my routine and turning toward God in the midst of busy preoccupation was itself a valuable aid.

This pattern of stopping for prayer several times a day is mentioned in the oldest of Christian documents outside the New Testament, the Didache (pronounced "DIDD-ah-kay"; it's also called "The Teaching of the Twelve Apostles"). The Didache was written in the late first century, perhaps about the same time as the Gospels of Matthew and Luke. It's an interesting text because it details what Christians do and don't do, and how they worship (it's a brief text; you can find it online). At one point, it provides the words of the "Our Father," and says that Christians should pray it three times a day. (It also mentions fasting on Wednesday and Friday.) So, if you are presently doing all your praying at one time of the day, you could use this opportunity of adding the Jesus Prayer to rearrange things, and divide your praying into two or more sessions. See if you benefit from that; it certainly improved things for me.

But maybe you don't already have a dedicated daily prayer time. You'll need to establish one, if you want to practice the Jesus Prayer in a formal and disciplined way. But some people do without a regular time to practice the Jesus Prayer, just employing it spontaneously during the day; we'll get to that option below.

When I first began trying to have a daily prayer time, decades ago, I decided that at 5:00 pm every day I would stop and pray for five minutes. *I thought I was going to jump out of my skin.* I hated it. I hated having to be still and focus on nothing but God, even for five minutes. So I know how hard this can be at first, and you have my sympathies. It does get easier with practice.

St. Gregory the Great (AD 540–604) said, "There is a great difference, dearly beloved brethren, between corporal and spiritual delights, in that the former, when we are without them, enkindle in the soul a strong desire to possess them, but once they are attained, they quickly satiate us. Spiritual pleasures, on the contrary, when unattained, produce a certain aversion; but once we taste them, the taste awakens desire, and our hunger for them increases the more we taste them."

If you've successfully added a good habit to your life before, you might be able to identify what helped you then and apply the same lesson here. I once read an article about the best way to form a new habit; the author had evaluated hundreds of "self-change techniques" and identified the three most effective methods. First, monitor yourself, and keep track of whether you meet your goal (for example, every day that you practice the Prayer, check it on your calendar). Second, commit to someone else that you will report your success or failure (a spiritual elder is ideal, but you could track success with a friend or family member instead). Third, make the new habit a convenient part of your daily routine. "Pin it" to something else that you do every day. Do you read the news every morning? When you sit down with the paper or at the computer, close your eyes and say the Jesus Prayer first. If you read your e-mail every day, say the Prayer after you sit at your desk but before you open your e-mail account. Pick something that is already an established habit, and embed this new practice into what you're already doing.

Be sincere in your prayers, whether you're saying the Jesus Prayer, participating in a church service, or saying private prayers at home. Don't ever let prayer become mere rote repetition. St. John of Kronstadt writes, "When you pray, the Lord will give you according to your heart. If you pray with faith, sincerely, with all your heart, not hypocritically, the Lord will reward you accordingly. And on the other hand, the colder your heart, the more doubting and hypocritical, the more useless will be your prayer—and more: so much the more will it insult the Lord, who seeks to be worshiped 'in spirit and truth'" (Jn. 4:23).[3]

Some people elect to undertake their daily practice of the Jesus Prayer as they're drifting off to sleep. This sounds like a good plan, because you won't feel pressured to hurry up and do something else, and you will be soothed and relieved of worries as you prepare for sleep. But personally, I resisted that option because I was afraid I'd forge an association between saying the

Prayer and getting sleepy. I was hoping (still am hoping) to one day really be able to pray without ceasing, and if my ingrained experience of the Jesus Prayer was pillow time, I would not learn how to employ it while alert and functioning. That was my thinking, anyway; I could be wrong. Whenever you do set up your daily prayer time, there's no reason you couldn't also use the Prayer as you're heading off to sleep.

The benefit of making this an ingrained habit will last all your life, outlasting, perhaps, even your conscious awareness. People who care for the elderly, and pastors who pray beside a deathbed, know that those who have journeyed far into dementia still respond when they hear something familiar that expresses their faith. A friend's mother was often afraid because she no longer recognized her surroundings, but would become quiet and be comforted when my friend opened the Bible and read favorite passages aloud. When my spiritual father, Fr. George Calciu (AD 1925–2006; he was, like Fr. Roman Braga, a survivor of torture in Communist prisons), was in his last hours, though he had long appeared insensible to those around him, he tried to sing along when a favorite hymn was begun, and struggled to lift his right hand to make the sign of the cross.

The things we lay down firmly in our memories *matter*. They endure. If you take the words of the Jesus Prayer and "write them on the tablet of your heart" (Prov. 3:3), on the day when you are far away on the gray sea of Alzheimer's, the Prayer will still be there, keeping your hand clasped in the hand of the Lord.

A nun had been assigned to care for an elderly monk with advanced dementia. One day his babbling was of a kind that was distressing to her. Suddenly he broke free, as it were, looked her in the eye and said, "Dear sister, you are upset because of what I am saying. But do not fear. Inside, I am with God."

The Jesus Prayer is rightly called a prayer discipline, because it entails hard work. St. Paul spoke of laboring with the Galatians "until Christ be formed in you" (Gal. 4:19). So I hope you're not disappointed to learn that there is no trick or shortcut to being able to pray constantly. What you have to do is: pray constantly. The Jesus Prayer offers a framework, a way to begin doing it.

It's encouraging to remember that it has met the test of time, and proven itself over more than fifteen hundred years.

The goal of saying the Jesus Prayer is not to say it *perfectly* for fifteen minutes a day. The goal is to pray constantly, and to practice is to lay a foundation of habit and familiarity for feeding the remainder of the day. If you don't feel called to spend time in formal practice, you could and should use the Prayer anyway, as you follow your everyday course. (Metropolitan Kallistos Ware calls these the "fixed use" and the "free use" of the Jesus Prayer.) Using the Prayer spontaneously, in all circumstances, brings the Lord into your life in a vivid way. Every task is done in his presence and with his help. Every encounter takes place under his loving gaze.

So, pray at all times, or at least at all the times you think of it. You can "pray constantly" apart from the Jesus Prayer, too. Sometimes we have more specific things to pray about, things we need to name; if so, it is right to converse with the Lord freely about everything on our mind, simply, like a child. It is all right to pray for help in finding a parking place. If it concerns us, it concerns him.

But over the years, our concerns become less anxious and self-centered, and we are able to loosen our grip on what we think we need to have. Priorities shift. If it concerns him, it will concern us. The Jesus Prayer provides a way to maintain a fluid connection through the day, as we listen to hear his will.

FOR FURTHER READING

OVERVIEW

Bajis, Jordan. *Common Ground: An Introduction to Eastern Orthodox Christianity for the American Christian*. Minneapolis: Light and Life Publishing, 1996.

Gillquist, Fr. Peter. *Becoming Orthodox*: A Journey to the Ancient Christian Faith. Ben Lomond, CA: Conciliar Press, 1992.

Hopko, Fr. Thomas. *The Orthodox Faith*. 4 vols. Brooklyn, OH: Orthodox Christian Publications Center, 1972.

Payton, James. *Light from the Christian East: An Introduction to the Orthodox Tradition*. Downers Grove, IL: Intervarsity Press, 2007.

Schmemann, Fr. Alexander. *The Historical Road of Eastern Orthodoxy*. Crestwood, NY: St. Vladimir's Seminary Press, 1977.

Ware, Bishop Kallistos. *The Orthodox Church*. London: Penguin Books, 1991.

THE JESUS PRAYER

Anonymous, *The Way of a Pilgrim* (many publishers).

Behr-Sigel, Elisabeth. *The Place of the Heart: An Introduction to Orthodox Spirituality*. Torrance, CA: Oakwood Publications, 1992.

Brianchaninov, St. Ignatius. *On the Prayer of Jesus*. Berwick, ME: Ibis Press, 2006.

Gillet, Fr. Lev, "A Monk of the Eastern Church." *The Jesus Prayer*. Crestwood, NY: St. Vladimir's Seminary Press, 1987.

Golynsky-Mihailovsky, Abp. Anthony, *Two Elders on the Jesus Prayer*. Edited and compiled by N. M. Novikov. Translated by Igor V. Ksenzov. Hayesville, OH: Skete of the Entrance of the Theotokos into the Temple, 2008.

Hausherr, Irénée. *The Name of Jesus*. Kalamazoo, MI: Cistercian Publications, 1978.

Igumen Chariton of Valamo, ed. *The Art of Prayer*. Translated by E. Kadloubovsky and E. M. Palmer. Boston: Faber & Faber, 1981.

EASTERN CHRISTIAN SPIRITUALITY & ASCETICISM

Bloom, Metropolitan Anthony. *Beginning to Pray*. New York: Paulist Press, 1970.

Braga, Fr. Roman. *Exploring the Inner Universe: Joy—the Mystery of Life*. Rives Junction, MI: Holy Dormition Monastery Press, 1996.

Brianchaninov, St. Ignatius. *The Arena*. Jordanville, NY: Holy Trinity Monastery, 1997.

Calciu, Fr. George. *Christ is Calling You! A Course in Catacomb Pastorship*. Forestville, CA: St. Herman of Alaska Brotherhood, 1998.

Colliander, Tito. *Way of the Ascetics: The Ancient Tradition of Discipline and Inner Growth*. Crestwood, NY: St. Vladimir's Seminary Press, 1985.

Evdokimov, Paul. *Ages of the Spiritual Life*. Crestwood, NY: St. Vladimir's Seminary Press, 1998.

Grisbrooke, W. Jardine, ed. *Spiritual Counsels of St. John of Kronstadt*. Crestwood, NY: St. Vladimir's Seminary Press, 1989.

Hausherr, Irénée. *Penthos: The Doctrine of Compunction in the Christian East*. Kalamazoo, MI: Cistercian Publications, 1982.

Hopko, Fr. Thomas. *The Lenten Spring: Readings for Great Lent*. Crestwood, NY: St. Vladimir's Seminary Press, 1983.

Logothetis, Archimandrite Spyridon. *The Heart: An Orthodox Christian Spiritual Guide*. Nafpakos, Greece: Holy Transfiguration Monastery, 2001.

Markides, Kyriacos. *The Mountain of Silence: A Search for Orthodox Spirituality*. New York: Doubleday, 2001.

Mathewes-Green, Frederica. *The Illumined Heart: The Ancient Christian Path of Transformation*. Brewster, MA: Paraclete Press, 2001.

Schmemann, Fr. Alexander. *For the Life of the World: Sacraments and Orthodoxy*. Crestwood, NY: St. Vladimir's Seminary Press, 1997.

Vlachos, Archimandrite Hierotheos. *The Illness and Cure of the Soul in the Orthodox Church*. Levadia, Greece: Holy Monastery of the Birth of the Theotokos, 2005.

———. *A Night in the Desert of the Holy Mountain: Discussion with a Hermit on the Jesus Prayer*. Levadia, Greece: Holy Monastery of the Birth of the Theotokos, 2003.

Ware, Bishop Kallistos. *The Orthodox Way*. Crestwood, NY: St. Vladimir's Seminary Press, 1995.

NOTES

1   Andreas Andreopoulos, *The Sign of the Cross* (Brewster, MA: Paraclete Press, 2006), 61.

2   Abp. Anthony Golynsky-Mihailovsky, *Two Elders on the Jesus Prayer*, ed. and comp. N. M. Novikov, trans. Igor V. Ksenzov (Hayesville, OH: Skete of the Entrance of the Theotokos into the Temple, 2008), 51.

3   W. Jardine Grisbrooke, ed., *Spiritual Counsels of St. John of Kronstadt* (Crestwood, NY: St. Vladimir's Seminary Press, 1989), 29–30.

About Paraclete Press

Who We Are

Paraclete Press is a publisher of books, recordings, and DVDs on Christian spirituality. Our publishing represents a full expression of Christian belief and practice—from Catholic to Evangelical, from Protestant to Orthodox.

We are the publishing arm of the Community of Jesus, an ecumenical monastic community in the Benedictine tradition. As such, we are uniquely positioned in the marketplace without connection to a large corporation and with informal relationships to many branches and denominations of faith.

What We Are Doing

Books

Paraclete publishes books that show the richness and depth of what it means to be Christian. Although Benedictine spirituality is at the heart of all that we do, we publish books that reflect the Christian experience across many cultures, time periods, and houses of worship. We publish books that nourish the vibrant life of the church and its people—books about spiritual practice, formation, history, ideas, and customs.

We have several different series, including the best-selling Paraclete Essentials, and Paraclete Giants series of classic texts in contemporary English; A Voice from the Monastery—men and women monastics writing about living a spiritual life today; award-winning literary faith fiction and poetry; and the Active Prayer Series that brings creativity and liveliness to any life of prayer.

Recordings

From Gregorian chant to contemporary American choral works, our music recordings celebrate sacred choral music through the centuries. Paraclete distributes the recordings of the internationally acclaimed choir Gloriæ Dei Cantores, praised for their "rapt and fathomless spiritual intensity" by *American Record Guide*, and the Gloriæ Dei Cantores Schola, which specializes in the study and performance of Gregorian chant. Paraclete is also the exclusive North American distributor of the recordings of the Monastic Choir of St. Peter's Abbey in Solesmes, France, long considered to be a leading authority on Gregorian chant.

DVDs

Our DVDs offer spiritual help, healing, and biblical guidance for life issues: grief and loss, marriage, forgiveness, anger management, facing death, and spiritual formation.

Learn more about us at our website:
www.paracletepress.com, or call us toll-free at 1-800-451-5006.

Ancient Spiritual Disciplines

In this new series of "little books" *you will learn how to grasp the meaning of ancient ways of praying in a relatively short amount of time. This will leave you with the rest of your life to move beyond the reading and into the practicing!*

PRAYING
with Icons

Linette Martin

64 pages ISBN: 1-978-1-61261-058-0
$24.95 (pack of 5), Small paperback

Available from most booksellers or
through Paraclete Press